AMAZING PLACES

4x5 DOOR

1x2x3 WALL ELEMENT

1x1x2 HINGE BRICK AND WINDOW SHUTTER

1x6 TILE

2x4 PLATE

2x2 TILE

2x2 TILE

2x3 PLATE

HOME ESSENTIALS
Door and window pieces are useful for building houses. Mix and match colors and styles if you don't have enough of one!

6x6 TILE

2x3 CURVED PLATE WITH HOLE

1x6 ARCHED FENCE

1x2x2 WINDOW FRAME

BUSH

FLOWER   **FLOWER**

DO IT YOURSELF!
If you haven't got a ready-made piece, try to recreate it yourself.

LUGGAGE CART

USE REAL BUILDINGS AS INSPIRATION. THEN ADD SOME IMAGINATION!

1x1 CORNER PANEL

FLOWER WITH OPEN STUD

BALL JOINT

CARROT   CHERRIES

BAMBOO PLANT

FLOWERS AND STEM

SMALL TREE

BARRED WINDOW WITH 2 CONNECTIONS

USE WHAT YOU HAVE
Be innovative with your bricks. If you don't have a ladder, turn this barred window (above) on its side! (See Children's Bedroom, p.9)

1x2 PLATE WITH SIDE RAIL

1x2 TEXTURED BRICK

CRATE

THE GREAT OUTDOORS
Remember to build both indoor and outdoor spaces to make your scene as realistic as possible.

LARGE PLANT LEAVES

FAUCET

TELESCOPE

ORNAMENTAL ARCH

1x4x2 LATTICE GATE

1x4x2 BARRED FENCE

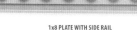

1x4x1 LATTICE FENCE

1x8 PLATE WITH SIDE RAIL

1x2 FAUCET

DRAWER

PIG

DETAILED BUILDING
Use ready-built pieces, like faucets, brooms, and animals to add detail to your scene.

SEAT

1x2 PRINTED TILE

BROOM

BE INVENTIVE
Try to come up with new uses for unusual pieces. This large radar dish (above) makes an excellent clock face. (See Clock Tower, p.14)

6x6 RADAR DISH

3x5 CURVED LEGO® TECHNIC HALF BEAM

2x2 ROUND PLATE

PALM TREE SEGMENT

2x2 CONE

MAILBOX WITH DOOR

CUPBOARD WITH DOOR

1x2 PLATE WITH BAR

LONG CHAIN

1x2 JUMPER PLATE

BRICKS FOR BUILDING

Town and country scenes have endless building potential. Look through your LEGO® collection and pick out pieces that will help you build walls, doors, windows, roofs, gardens, and whatever else you can imagine in your LEGO world! These pieces are a good place to start, but there's no limit to the bricks you can use in your creations.

1x3x2 HALF ARCH

1x2 RIDGED ROOF CORNER SLOPE

1x1 BRICK WITH 2 SIDE STUDS

1x1 HEADLIGHT BRICK

LEGO TECHNIC HALF PIN

1x2 BRICK WITH 2 HOLES

1x5 ANGLED BRICK

1x4 BRICK WITH SIDE STUDS

2x2 BRICK

1x2 BRICK

LINES AND CURVES
Choose bricks with interesting shapes, like arches and curves, so that your buildings aren't always square!

2x4 RIDGED ROOF SLOPE

1x6 TILE

2x3 SLOPE

1x2 CURVED HALF ARCH

3x8 ANGLED PLATE

1x12x3 ARCHED BRICK

1x2x3 INVERTED SLOPE

6x8 RAMP

FAMILY HOUSE

Town construction is all about making detailed models of real buildings—and what could be better than making a home for an entire LEGO family? Plan out your bricks before you start, to see which colors you have the most of. Do you want matching doors and windows? Two floors or three? This is your house—the design is up to you!

BUILDING BRIEF
Objective: Build big family houses
Use: Sleeping, cooking, living, dining
Features: Must be strong and sturdy, removable roof
Extras: Furniture, satellite dish, front and back yards

HOUSE BUILDING

Start your house with a basic brick outline, and decide where you want to put the doors and windows before you make the walls. Plan the layouts of your rooms as you build so everybody has enough space—and remember, you'll want to add furniture, so leave space for that, too!

If you don't have enough roof pieces and slopes, use plates and hinges to build an opening roof!

You could make each floor a different color

SURE, I'LL REBUILD THE HOUSE THIS WEEKEND!

YOU'LL HAVE TO ASK YOUR FATHER, DEAR.

CAN'T I HAVE A BIGGER ROOM? PLEEEAAASE?

Garden—use flowers, trees, and colorful 1x1 plates to design your outdoor space

There are many different types of doors and windows. Will you stick to one style for your family house—or mix and match?

Real lawns aren't totally flat, so use a few plates to add depth

You could build a bigger yard, and add sheds, swings, or even a swimming pool!

EASY ACCESS

Make each floor removable by lining the tops of the walls with tiles. Use just a few plates with exposed studs to hold the next level in place.

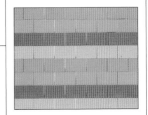

Inner walls built into outer walls for strength to support upper levels

EXPLODED VIEW

Choose where to place your staircase before finalizing the room layout

Each row of roof tiles is supported by a layer of bricks underneath

Each floor is about seven or eight bricks high

Textured bricks add detail and decoration

Balcony railing made from barred fence

BRICKS IN THE WALL

If you don't have enough of one color, build walls with stripes or other patterns. You could try to replicate the look of real bricks —or use crazy colors!

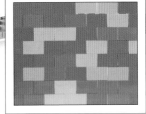

Front walkway, built with tiles. You could add a welcome mat, too!

GROUND FLOOR

What does a minifigure family need? Take a look at real houses to decide what rooms and furniture you want. The ground floors of most houses have a foyer, dining room, and kitchen, but maybe you want to build a playroom or den as well?

Bookshelf. The sides are made from curved LEGO® Technic half beams

Table lamp, built from just two pieces

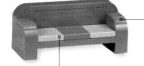

Curved pieces make furniture look soft

LIVING ROOM

Stretch out the middle of a comfy chair and you've got a family couch!

Shiny wood floor, made with tiles. You could add a rug, using colored pieces, or a thick carpet, using studs

DINING ROOM

Cabinet drawers with handles, made from jumper plates

Make extra tile tablecloths for special occasions

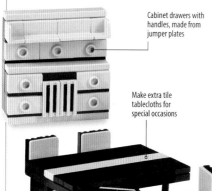

Table legs made from telescopes

THIS PLACE HAS EVERYTHING PLUS THE KITCHEN SINK!

KITCHEN

Stove, built from a mailbox and two printed videotape tiles

FURNITURE

When building furniture, look at your pieces in new ways. Turn them around or upside-down and see if you can discover part of a chair, lamp, or sofa. Remember to build your furniture to minifigure scale!

STAIRS

The stairs in this house use a long rubber piece for the handrail, supported by skeleton legs. If you don't have these pieces, you could use 1x1 bricks in alternating colors and 1x1 slopes.

TOP FLOOR

Every member of the family is an individual, so all the bedrooms in the house should be distinct, too. Make each one show the interests and personality of whoever sleeps there. You could also put in a guest room, storage room, or games room!

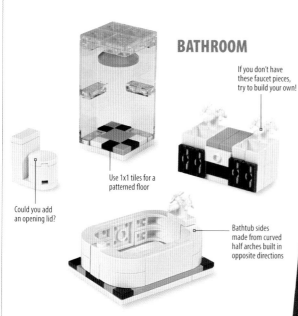

BATHROOM

If you don't have these faucet pieces, try to build your own!

Use 1x1 tiles for a patterned floor

Could you add an opening lid?

Bathtub sides made from curved half arches built in opposite directions

TOP FLOOR FURNITURE

When you're building the same piece of furniture a few times, try to make each item unique. Experiment with sizes, colors, and styles, and think about how a child's furniture is different from an adult's!

Master bedroom doors open out onto balcony

Long tiles create wooden plank effect

LAMPS

Modern floor lamp made with two radar dishes and an antenna

Crystal lamp base made with transparent plates

For stability, build the balcony directly into the floor of the top story

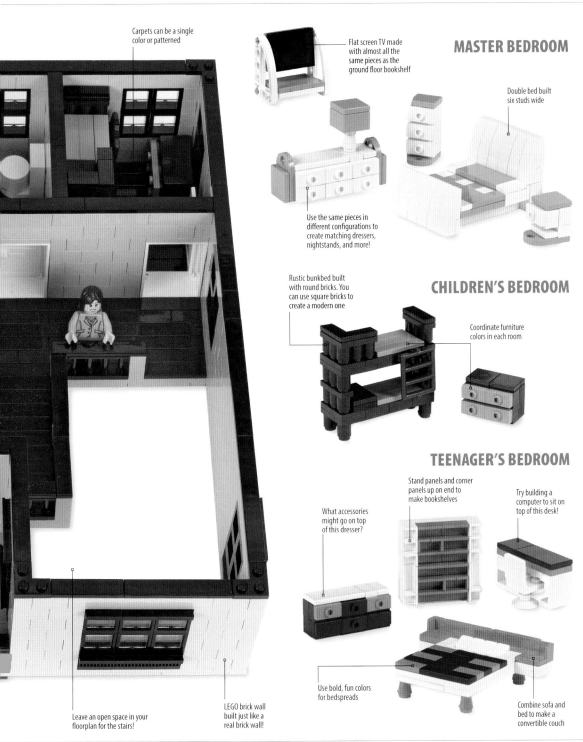

Carpets can be a single color or patterned

Flat screen TV made with almost all the same pieces as the ground floor bookshelf

MASTER BEDROOM

Double bed built six studs wide

Use the same pieces in different configurations to create matching dressers, nightstands, and more!

Rustic bunkbed built with round bricks. You can use square bricks to create a modern one

CHILDREN'S BEDROOM

Coordinate furniture colors in each room

TEENAGER'S BEDROOM

Stand panels and corner panels up on end to make bookshelves

Try building a computer to sit on top of this desk!

What accessories might go on top of this dresser?

Use bold, fun colors for bedspreads

Combine sofa and bed to make a convertible couch

Leave an open space in your floorplan for the stairs!

LEGO brick wall built just like a real brick wall!

MICROBUILDINGS

Want to build a whole town or city, but don't have much space? Try creating microbuildings! With just a handful of standard bricks, a few special pieces here and there, and lots of imagination, you can build a landscape that is tiny, but hugely impressive!

LIGHT AND COLOR

Use transparent plates to create the look of stained-glass windows. You may not be able to capture the intricate detail of the real thing, but the idea will shine through!

1x1 slopes look more in-scale than big roof pieces

Simple color scheme

Add details to break up plain facades

Small arched frame becomes a giant door

GRAND BUILDING

The scale of your building will sometimes be determined by the best piece for the job. This cathedral-inspired model is built to fit the scale of small arched windows!

RAISE THE ROOF

The building's roof is built up one row at a time using 1x1 slopes, arranged in a simple pattern. Each row is one plate higher than the last one.

1x1 green cones make great hedges and trees

Building fronts don't have to be angular—try using curved slopes

Textured bricks add detail

CANAL HOUSE

Photographs can help you design locations from a particular time or place, like this Dutch canal house. Keep the proportions as close as possible to the real thing.

STREET STORES

For a row of buildings, start with a street base, made of plates and tiles. Create each building separately and then attach it to the base. Give each one its own distinct lines, like the green and orange store's curved roof.

Try to choose interesting color combinations

Add awnings and overhangs to entrances

Building and trim have contrasting colors

REAR VIEW

Add simple decorative details, but don't overdo it

MICROHOUSE

Don't just build a boring box for your microscale house. Experiment with different shapes and pieces! Pick out your windows and doors first so you know how big to make the rest of the building around them.

Windows make great doors at microscale

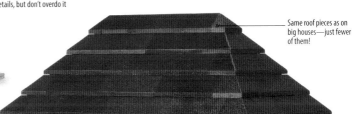

Same roof pieces as on big houses—just fewer of them!

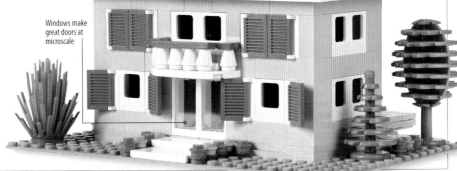

TRAIN STATION

A train station is a functional building, but that doesn't mean it has to look boring! Try to design your station in an unusual shape, and give it some interesting features, like arched doorways, striking brickwork, or a unique roof. You could even build a removable roof so you can access the interior for rebuilding and play.

BUILDING BRIEF
Objective: Build train stations
Use: A place for passengers to get tickets and wait for their trains
Features: Ticket desk, indoor and outdoor waiting areas
Extras: Trains, signal lights, signs, train tracks

GETTING INTO SHAPE

Building a roof in an unusual shape can be tricky, so focus on this aspect of the model first. When the roof is complete, build the walls to fit.

Roof built in an elongated hexagonal shape

I'M LATE! DO LEGO TRAINS RUN ON TIME?

ARCHES

Two half arches form the top of a fancy doorway, while a single half arch piece can be used to support part of the roof.

Elevate the main building on a platform to draw attention to it

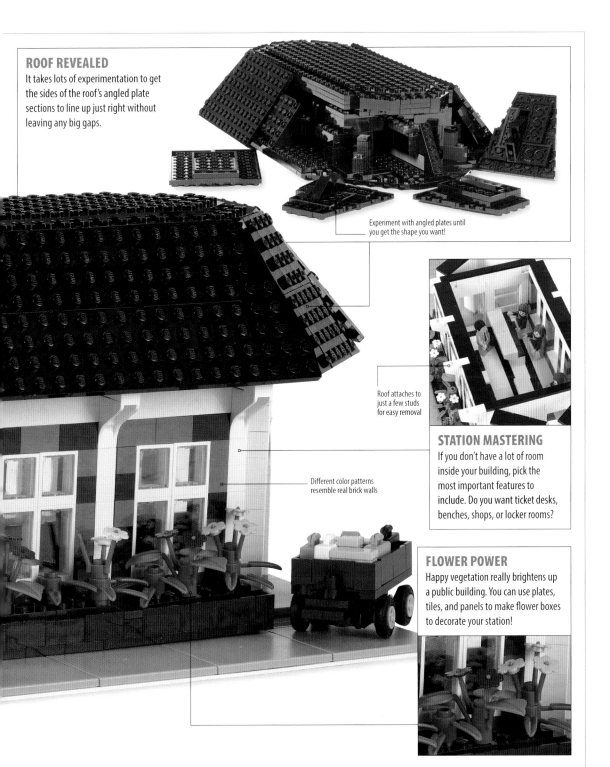

ROOF REVEALED

It takes lots of experimentation to get the sides of the roof's angled plate sections to line up just right without leaving any big gaps.

Experiment with angled plates until you get the shape you want!

Roof attaches to just a few studs for easy removal

Different color patterns resemble real brick walls

STATION MASTERING

If you don't have a lot of room inside your building, pick the most important features to include. Do you want ticket desks, benches, shops, or locker rooms?

FLOWER POWER

Happy vegetation really brightens up a public building. You can use plates, tiles, and panels to make flower boxes to decorate your station!

STATION BUILDINGS

It takes more than one building to make a train station! Look at real stations to get ideas about what else your scene could include. Each building should be different from the others, but perhaps you could incorporate common elements into each of them so they all fit together.

BUILDING BRIEF
Objective: Make more buildings for your train station
Use: Keeping the trains on schedule
Features: Matching color schemes, useful station functions
Extras: A method of connecting the buildings together

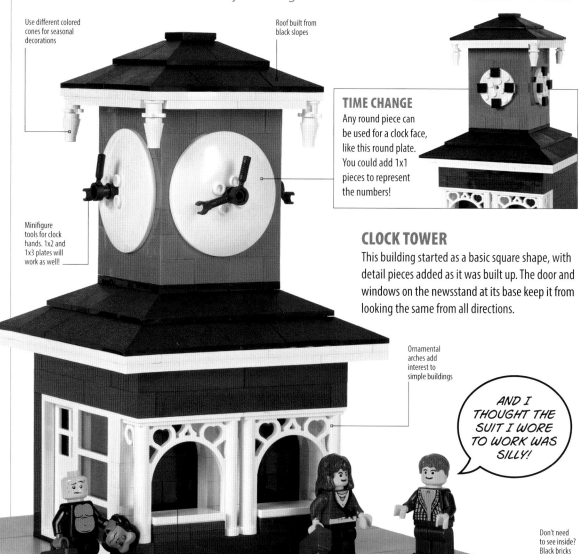

Use different colored cones for seasonal decorations

Roof built from black slopes

TIME CHANGE
Any round piece can be used for a clock face, like this round plate. You could add 1x1 pieces to represent the numbers!

Minifigure tools for clock hands. 1x2 and 1x3 plates will work as well!

CLOCK TOWER
This building started as a basic square shape, with detail pieces added as it was built up. The door and windows on the newsstand at its base keep it from looking the same from all directions.

Ornamental arches add interest to simple buildings

AND I THOUGHT THE SUIT I WORE TO WORK WAS SILLY!

Don't need to see inside? Black bricks create the look of a dark interior

For extra playability, make the roof removable and add a control office inside

Half arch pieces

I'M NOT GREAT AT REPAIRS, BUT I LOVE WEARING THIS HARD HAT!

Tiles across the front of the railings hold them securely

SIGNAL TOWER

This building lets the railroad crew observe and control the movement of the trains and tracks. Because the top section is bigger than the bottom, half arches are attached to support it where they meet.

Use plates with side rails to make a windowsill. You could also add flowers

Brick with side stud

LEGO Technic half pin

STAIR SIDES

The railing panels are built with plates and tiles and then attached to the stairs using bricks with side studs and LEGO Technic half pins. To make the staircase extra stable, add a turn like this one.

15

INSIDE THE STATION

There are lots of great things you can build inside your train station, from rows of seats and departures desks, to check-in counters and x-ray scanning machines. You could also build waiting rooms, machines, and ticket counters for a bus station—or even an airport. Now all you need to do is get your minifigures ready to travel!

DEPARTURES

This is the departure gate, where passengers hand over their tickets before boarding the train. The simple desk is made from red and white pieces, with no sideways building.

You could use transparent pieces to cover the studs and act as desk lights

BUT I CAN'T SIT NEXT TO HER— WE'RE WEARING THE SAME TORSO!

This ticket counter could also be an airport check-in desk!

TICKET COUNTER

White bricks with tiles on top make this ticket counter look sleek and hi-tech. Computer screens are positioned at an angle on jumper plates, and the keyboards are attached with a clip and bar hinge so they can be positioned at an angle.

You could build the computer desks in the colors of your railway company

Same-color minifigure torsos look like uniforms

SITTING AROUND

Build your waiting area for as many passengers as you like. These red seats clip onto a 2x12 plate. The feet are 1x2 jumper plates with 1x1 round plates on top. Don't forget to add a small side table. Remember: it's all about the details!

SORRY, BUT MY THREE INVISIBLE FRIENDS ARE SITTING HERE.

2x2 tile used as tabletop

Jumper plates evenly spaced out

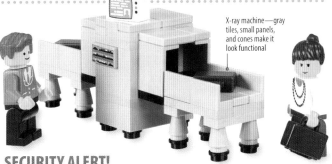

X-ray machine—gray tiles, small panels, and cones make it look functional

Keyboards and computer screens can be found in various LEGO® City sets, but you could use a plain tile or a grille instead

SECURITY ALERT!

Security is an important feature in airports and some train and bus stations. Make sure your x-ray machine is the right size to scan LEGO luggage, and that the body scanner is tall enough for a minifigure—and his hat—to walk through!

X-ray scanner, made from specialized angled pieces. A stack of 1x2 bricks with slopes on the top corners would work just as well

COUNTRY BARN

Want a break from the hustle and bustle of the big city? Head out to the countryside and build yourself a farm, starting with a good old-fashioned barn. Make it big and sturdy, with plenty of room for animals, crops, and equipment inside. Farming life is hard work, but building it can be lots of fun!

BARN RAISING

The roof is the trickiest part of this model, so build it first, leaving a narrow groove in the underside so it can slot securely onto the barn walls and be removed easily. Match the trim around the doors and windows to the colors of the roof.

Weather vane—try different animals on top, too!

Use 1x3 slopes for the upper roof and 1x2 slopes for the lower roof to get a perfect barn shape!

Vary shape and size of windows

Don't have enough slopes for roof tiles? Use plates instead!

With winch parts, you could make the hayloft crane really work

AHHH...DON'T YOU JUST LOVE THAT FRESH COUNTRY AIR?

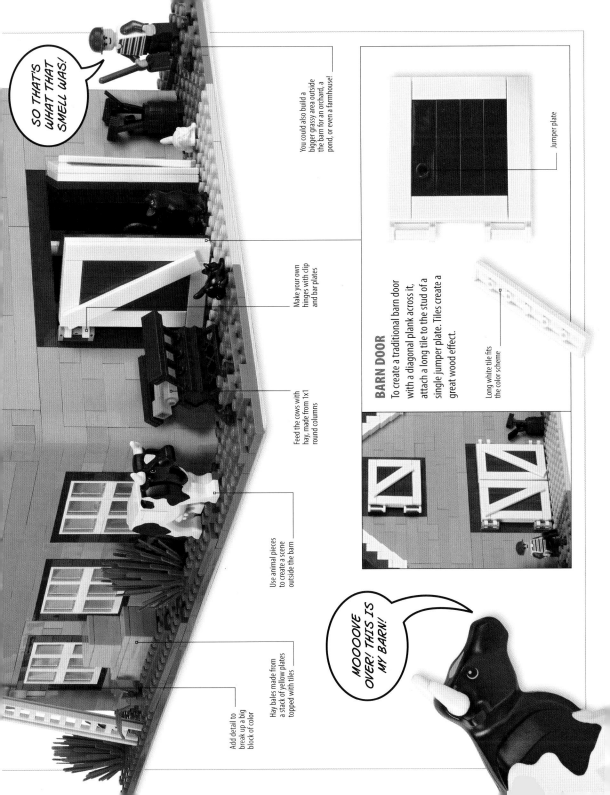

SO THAT'S WHAT THAT SMELL WAS!

You could also build a bigger grassy area outside the barn for an orchard, a pond, or even a farmhouse!

Jumper plate

Make your own hinges with clip and bar plates

BARN DOOR

To create a traditional barn door with a diagonal plank across it, attach a long tile to the stud of a single jumper plate. Tiles create a great wood effect.

Long white tile fits the color scheme

Feed the cows with hay, made from 1x1 round columns

Use animal pieces to create a scene outside the barn

Hay bales made from a stack of yellow plates topped with tiles

Add detail to break up a big block of color

MOOOOVE OVER! THIS IS MY BARN!!

FARMYARD LIFE

With the right bricks and pieces, you can create a whole farm for those hard-working minifigures. Think about what kind of farm you want to run—a dairy farm, an orchard, a ranch—and bring it to life!

BUILDING BRIEF
Objective: Build whole farms
Use: Milking, sowing, feeding, harvesting
Features: Coops, pens, orchards, natural surroundings
Extras: Tractor, field, stable, pen, farmer's house

Some duck houses are built on an island in the middle of a pond. Where will yours go?

COOL COVER

The angled roof of this duck house is made from large ramp pieces, which are built up and locked together with basic plates. You could even attach the roof with a clip and bar hinge so you can play inside!

HOLD ON? THIS IS NICER THAN *MY* HOUSE!

BRICK FOWL

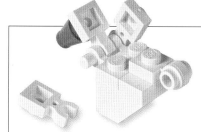

If you don't have the right LEGO animal, make your own! This duck is made using a few simple colors and pieces, like clip-plate wings and a bill made from a 1x1 cone.

DUCK HOUSE

A duck house doesn't have to be a plain, white hut! Design an unusual roof, add lattice windows, or build it on a raised platform so the ducks can wander underneath.

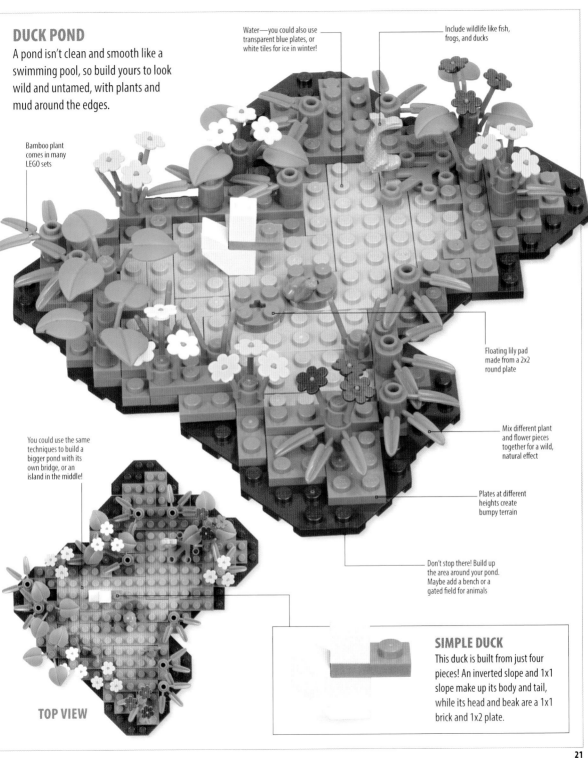

DUCK POND

A pond isn't clean and smooth like a swimming pool, so build yours to look wild and untamed, with plants and mud around the edges.

Water—you could also use transparent blue plates, or white tiles for ice in winter!

Include wildlife like fish, frogs, and ducks

Bamboo plant comes in many LEGO sets

Floating lily pad made from a 2x2 round plate

You could use the same techniques to build a bigger pond with its own bridge, or an island in the middle!

Mix different plant and flower pieces together for a wild, natural effect

Plates at different heights create bumpy terrain

Don't stop there! Build up the area around your pond. Maybe add a bench or a gated field for animals

TOP VIEW

SIMPLE DUCK

This duck is built from just four pieces! An inverted slope and 1x1 slope make up its body and tail, while its head and beak are a 1x1 brick and 1x2 plate.

DOWN ON THE FARM

To bring your farm creations to life, think about the small details: What does a shed's roof really look like? How can you build a realistic gate? What fruit will be growing in your orchard? Don't stop until you're really happy with your model!

TIN ROOF

Long, gray plates with side-rails look like a sheet of corrugated metal when attached side-by-side.

Roof is attached to shed with a 1x6 jumper plate

A plate hung diagonally adds decoration

THAT'S A WHOLE LOTTA FARM TO WATER. I'LL NEED A BIGGER CAN.

TOOL SHED

To make your doors (or windows) look smaller than they are, build a doorway the size you want, then place the door behind it so it opens inward.

DON'T HOG ALL THE FOOD, HAMLET!

A clean, square fence on rough, uneven terrain makes a good visual contrast

PIGPEN

You don't want farm animals to run wild and eat your crops, so build some enclosures! Instead of a single-piece base, this sty has layers of plates to give its surface some depth.

Mud doesn't stay inside boundaries, so let it flow out past the fence

Gate made from lattice gate attached upside-down

BRICK FRUIT

If you don't have pieces of LEGO fruit, make your own! Round or square red bricks make great apples, or use yellow for lemons. Can you think of any other pieces to use?

You could add flowers to your trees, too!

Palm tree segments come in many LEGO sets—or you could use round bricks

ORCHARD

You could build a well-tended orchard with rows of straight, matching trees—but your farm will look more natural if your tree trunks and branches are different shapes.

Build a strong, wide base to support a tall tree

If it's fall, your tree may have fewer leaves on it

Why not build a whole vegetable patch with rows of lettuces, carrots, and tomatoes?

Carrot growing out of the ground is really a 1x1 brick topped with a 2x2 plate!

2x2 round plate

EASY AS ONE, TWO, TREE

Building your own trees is easy! Stack round brown bricks or plates on a sturdy base for the trunk, then add plant leaves or any green pieces as leaves.

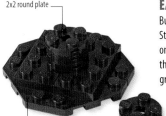

Use green plates if you want your tree to have a base of grass

CASTLE

Medieval castles are huge, sturdy structures. Other than that, you can build your model however you want: grand, ornate, plain, strong, majestic, or crumbling. You could even build it as a combination of all these things! Look at pictures of ancient castles, or find inspiration in your favorite books and movies. Think about including details like flags, wall-mounted torches, and knight minifigures to bring your creation to life.

BUILDING BRIEF
Objective: Build medieval castles
Use: Home for royalty and knights, defending the village, location of jewels and treasure
Features: Must be big and strong, able to withstand attack, majestic architecture
Extras: Interior rooms, inner courtyards, drawbridge, moat, gardens, a whole town within the castle walls

ARCHITECTURE

An interesting architectural feature can really give your model a boost. Here, a smaller arch has been built in behind a larger arch, which adds depth and detail to the chapel walls. Cones, round bricks, and round plates are stacked to make decorative columns. Be inventive!

Some parts of the castle can be very ornate, even if others are plain. Cones, tiles, and side stud pieces can create imposing sculptures

CURVED BATTLEMENTS

Rounded battlements can help your knights keep a lookout in all directions. Use hinged plates to connect several sections of wall together. Then angle the walls into a circle, semicircle, or whatever shape you want.

Hinged plates

CASTLE FORTRESS

Castles are built up over time as each king or queen adds what he or she needs. Start with an impressive doorway and a grand central building. Then add on sections to house sleeping quarters, viewing platforms, dining rooms, chapels, stores, and anything else you can think of. They don't even have to match!

Different sections can be built from different materials. Use brown bricks for wooden walls and gray for stone

Log bricks are great for medieval building

Fly flags in your army's colors. You could also display shields or printed tiles to identify your king or queen

This castle even has a chapel attached

Arched windows. If you haven't got arched bricks, use half arches or inverted slopes

Arrow slits made from bricks with cross axle holes

A green brick here and there looks like a moss-covered stone!

Bricks in different shades of gray, textured bricks, and jog bricks help break up large stone walls

Green baseplate is a good starting point, but why don't you try building your castle on a hill, or on an island in the middle of a lake?

Scattered plates and tiles look like fallen ruins

Overgrown foliage suggests an old castle. You could build a well-tended garden instead

Imposing entrance. You could also add a gatehouse with a way to keep invaders out! (See pp.26–27)

Wooden structures with lattice windows look really medieval!

DRAWBRIDGES

Every castle needs protection from invading armies. First build a simple gatehouse as an imposing front to your fortification. Then, think about how best you want to defend your castle and design a mechanism to suit. You could create a portcullis, a heavy stone door, or a drawbridge. Here are two clever ways to build a drawbridge!

BUILDING BRIEF
Objective: Build drawbridges for your castle
Use: Protecting the castle's entrance
Features: A mechanism to open and close
Extras: Decorations, guards, defenses

Crank controls drawbridge

OPEN   **CLOSED**

GATEHOUSE

A simple gatehouse can be the first point of protection for your castle. Gray bricks and LEGO Technic half pins on either side of the door attach the drawbridge.

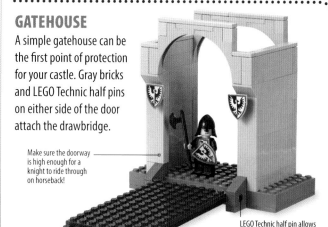

Make sure the doorway is high enough for a knight to ride through on horseback!

LEGO Technic half pin allows drawbridge to pivot

Push lever to release gears and send drawbridge crashing down!

MEDIEVAL MECHANISM

LEGO Technic gears turn to raise the lift-arms. These pull the chains, raising the drawbridge. A lever secures the drawbridge in place by locking an axle connector against the gears.

CRANK DRAWBRIDGE

A crank system is a simple way to raise and lower a drawbridge. This mechanism is housed in a stone battlement that connects to the top of the gatehouse. It uses LEGO Technic bricks, axles, and gears that allow you to operate the drawbridge using a crank on the side of the building.

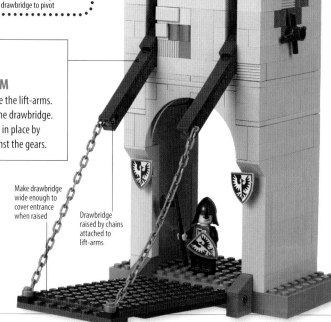

Make drawbridge wide enough to cover entrance when raised

Drawbridge raised by chains attached to lift-arms

CABLE DRAWBRIDGE

There's more than one way to raise a bridge! This version of the gatehouse uses a spool and string cable system instead of chains and lift-arms. The mechanism is housed in a rustic-style gatehouse room.

CLIPPING THE CABLES

Use plates with handled bars to secure your drawbridge's cables. Thread the cable through both handles before clipping them to the underside of the drawbridge.

Winch

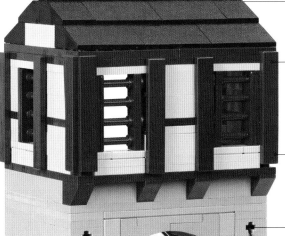

Not enough gray bricks? Build the top of your gatehouse using wood colors instead!

Hand-cranked winch is not as fast as a gear system, but it gets the job done!

SPOOL SYSTEM

The cables are attached to a winch inside the gatehouse, which is turned by a handle on the outside. This system takes up little space, which leaves room in the gatehouse for guards and ammunition.

Use a brick with cross axle hole in it to feed the cables through

Winch

CLOSED

OPEN

Don't have LEGO Technic parts? Use hinged bricks or plates to build a movable drawbridge

Plate with handled bar

BRIDGES

It's easy to snap some plates together and call it a bridge, but if you really want to cross a gap with style, try making a bridge that looks like the real thing—and works like it, too. Here's a great way to build a gentle humpback bridge for a park or country river crossing.

HUMPBACK BRIDGE

To build this picturesque bridge, start with a central arch. Make a solid base around the arch shape, building steps into it to create height. Then use slopes and tiles to create a smooth finish.

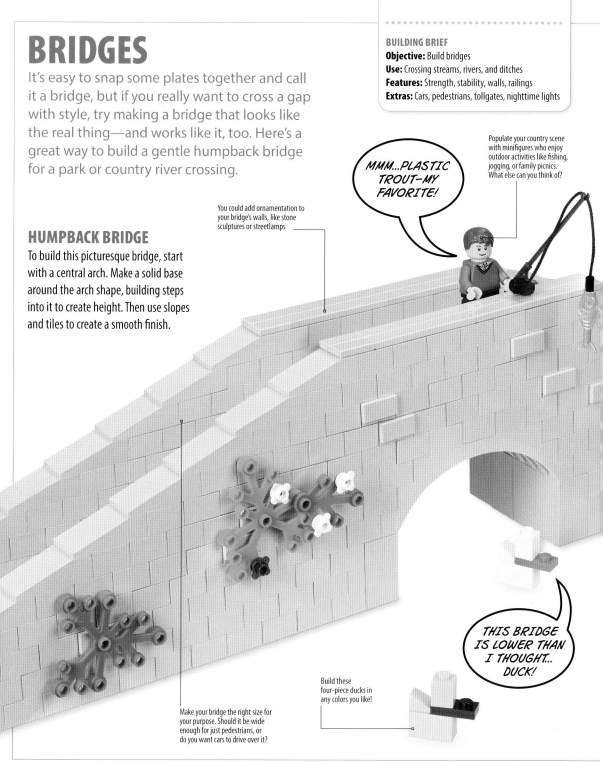

You could add ornamentation to your bridge's walls, like stone sculptures or streetlamps

Populate your country scene with minifigures who enjoy outdoor activities like fishing, jogging, or family picnics. What else can you think of?

MMM...PLASTIC TROUT—MY FAVORITE!

THIS BRIDGE IS LOWER THAN I THOUGHT... DUCK!

Make your bridge the right size for your purpose. Should it be wide enough for just pedestrians, or do you want cars to drive over it?

Build these four-piece ducks in any colors you like!

MINI ARCH

The arch is built just like the ones on the big model, but with fewer bricks. Use smaller arch pieces for even tinier bridges.

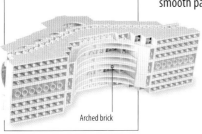

Arched brick

MICROBRIDGE

You can build a bridge in microscale, too! Try to include all the key features of a bigger model, like arches, support columns, railings, and a smooth pathway across.

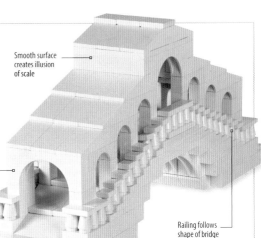

Smooth surface creates illusion of scale

All-white bricks look like polished marble

Railing follows shape of bridge

Use slopes to make the walls follow a gentle curve. You could also use plates to build gradual steps

You could also make a base for your bridge to sit on. Build it up with grass, trees flowers, and a river

Attach plant leaves and flowers to jumper plates built into the bridge walls

Your bridge doesn't have to be built out of tan bricks. Use brown pieces for a rustic wooden bridge, or gray for old stone

BULGING BRICKS

To make some of the stones bulge out from your wall, include headlight bricks among your 1x2 bricks and attach 1x2 tiles to them.

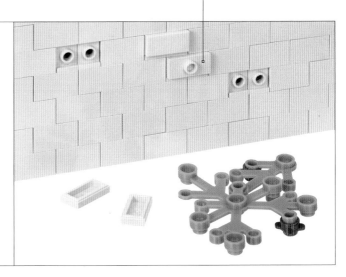

BIGGER BRIDGES

For larger spans of water, you need a bigger bridge! Large bridges usually have more arches to support their length and weight. They're made out of the strongest materials around, so use lots of gray bricks to mimic stone, or LEGO Technic pieces for metal girders.

Chains built into sides of pillars

If you don't have chains, use strings with studs, or build railings with bars

Create details to add decoration to your bridge

Archway tall enough for boats to pass below

CITY BRIDGE

The dimensions of the bridge are determined by the size of the key pieces and features, like the length of the chains and how wide the road needs to be to accommodate two lanes of traffic plus sidewalks. So build the road section first and then construct the arches underneath.

Add more bricks to make supports taller!

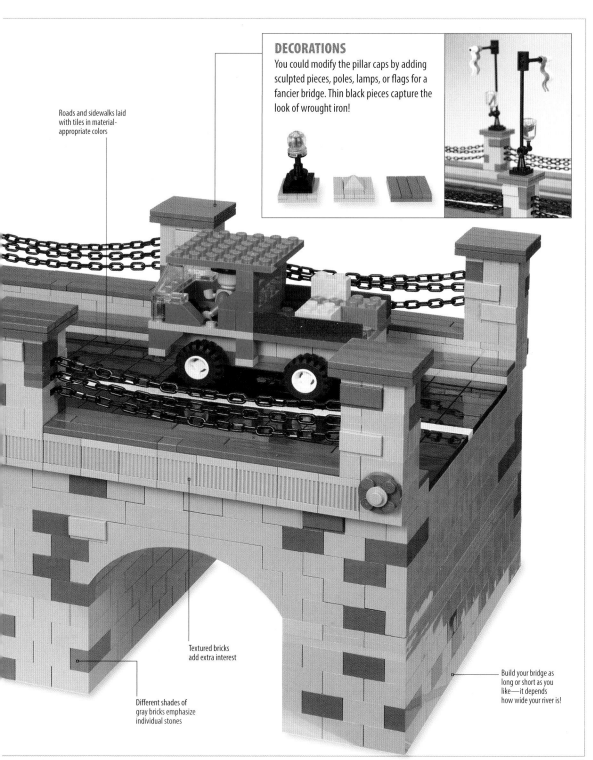

Roads and sidewalks laid with tiles in material-appropriate colors

DECORATIONS

You could modify the pillar caps by adding sculpted pieces, poles, lamps, or flags for a fancier bridge. Thin black pieces capture the look of wrought iron!

Textured bricks add extra interest

Different shades of gray bricks emphasize individual stones

Build your bridge as long or short as you like—it depends how wide your river is!

JUNGLE ROPE BRIDGE

You may never have been to a jungle, but everyone knows what they look like. Lots of green leaves, plants, and vines. Ancient, twisted trees. Rivers and waterfalls. There are so many possibilities! And when you create the natural world in bricks, you can be as freeform as you like—if you haven't got enough pieces to finish a tree, leave it as a stump!

BUILDING BRIEF
Objective: Create jungle scenes
Use: Exploration, adventure, discovery
Features: River, hanging bridge
Extras: Foliage, ladders, flowers

Vegetation, placed on irregular tree surfaces for a natural effect

String passes through the middle slat so the rope bridge keeps its shape. It hangs loose elsewhere

This is a great piece to make a jungle vine, which only needs one stud. You could also build clips into your tree to attach extra plants

ROPE BRIDGE

The coolest way to cross a jungle river is by rope bridge! This one is made from four lengths of string with studs on the ends. The slats are brown 1x4 plates. The trees are made from bricks, inverted slopes, and plant leaves, arranged to look random and natural, with lumps and bumps all over.

Bumpy forest floor, created using brown and green plates arranged in an irregular pattern

Access to the bridge is via a ladder, attached to the tree with a plate with handled bar

FALLEN LOGS

Logs fall on the forest floor and plants grow around them. Side branches may also have leaves growing from them. These leaves grow in different directions, which is what this model is replicating.

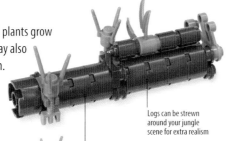

Logs can be strewn around your jungle scene for extra realism

1x1 round bricks form side branch

2x2 round brick

1x1 plate with horizontal clip

CLIP-ON LEAVES

The central trunk of the log is made from brown 2x2 round bricks. Then, a 1x1 plate with horizontal clip is fitted in so the plants can grow upward from the trunk.

CAMP FIRE

Here's a camp fire for cooking or warmth—even the jungle can get cold at night. Brown 1x1 round bricks form the logs and robot arms and tube studs hold the flames.

If you don't have flames, you could create smoldering embers with any small red and orange pieces

Palm tree leaves come in many LEGO sets

PALM TREES

The trunks of palm trees often have a natural bend, which can be recreated in bricks using various pieces. Any round brown bricks or cones would work, topped with leaves.

Specialized palm tree segment

INTO THE JUNGLE

Time to expand your jungle landscape! You can add mystery and adventure by building ancient ruins, and long-lost forbidden temples. Not everything has to be man-made, either—how about a raging river full of snapping crocodiles or a rushing waterfall? Go wild with your creations!

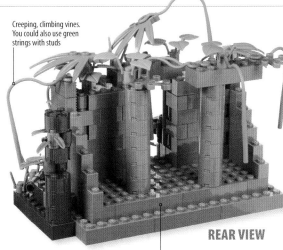

Creeping, climbing vines. You could also use green strings with studs

REAR VIEW

You could build trapdoors or tile mosaics into the floor

BUILDING BRIEF

Objective: Expand your jungle

Use: New places to play and explore

Features: Crumbling ruins, waterfalls

Extras: Jungle animals, trees, mountains

Mix different types of leaves and plants for an overgrown look

JUNGLE RUIN

To create an old, crumbling building, leave some of the walls incomplete so they look like they've fallen apart over the centuries. Creeping vines and other greenery show the jungle growing back over the ruins!

Gray pieces with unusual shapes or textures are good for old stone architecture

Stacked round bricks and leaves make broken tree trunks

Contrasting colors create eye-catching details

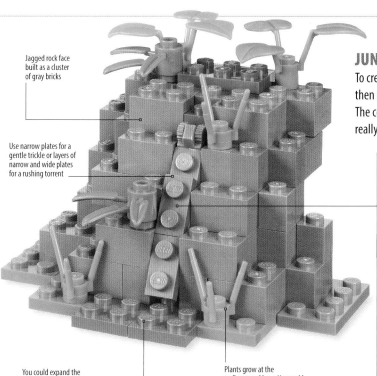

Jagged rock face built as a cluster of gray bricks

Use narrow plates for a gentle trickle or layers of narrow and wide plates for a rushing torrent

JUNGLE WATERFALL

To create a waterfall, first build a rocky base, then add blue bricks for running water. The coolest part is making it look like it's really flowing downhill.

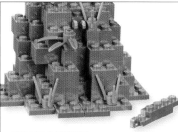

You could expand the pool at the bottom and create a jungle lake scene

Plants grow at the well-watered base. You could add flowers or trees, too!

FALLING WATER

The stream of this waterfall is made with one-stud-wide blue plates built onto plates with click hinges. Hinges allow the waterfall to be angled so it flows down the rocks. If you don't have hinges, try building the blue pieces directly onto the rock face.

GRAND ENTRANCE

The temple gate is built from a barred fence turned sideways. It is clipped to an antenna that is secured in the doorway. Use a plate with handled bar for the door handle.

Plate with handled bar

You can build the temple as large as you want!

You could completely cover your temple with vegetation and vines so it looks lost and forgotten

LOST TEMPLE

Even a small jungle building can make a big impact. This secret temple may look like an ordinary pile of rocks, but the barred gate hints that something important is hidden inside. What that is...is up to you!

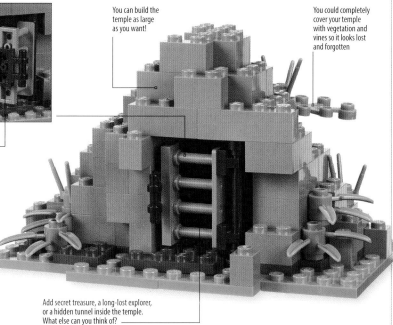

Add secret treasure, a long-lost explorer, or a hidden tunnel inside the temple. What else can you think of?

SHIPWRECK

Why not give your minifigures a pirate shipwreck scene to play in? You'll need a stormy sea, some ruinous rocks, and a pirate ship smashed to smithereens! Think of what else you could add to the scene—perhaps some floating treasure or escaping prisoners? You could even build a rowboat to rescue any survivors!

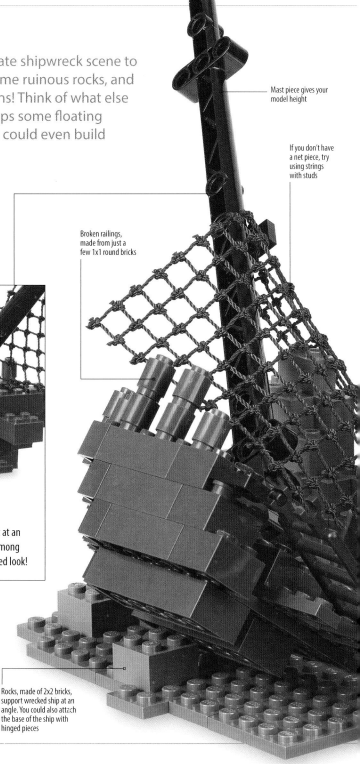

Mast piece gives your model height

If you don't have a net piece, try using strings with studs

Broken railings, made from just a few 1x1 round bricks

Rocks, made of 2x2 bricks, support wrecked ship at an angle. You could also attach the base of the ship with hinged pieces

BUILDING BRIEF

Objective: Build shipwreck scenes
Use: A scene to pose or play with your pirate crew
Features: Wrecked ship, rocks, water
Extras: Seagulls, waves, floating debris

Ladder piece. You could also add other debris, like a seat or a ship's steering wheel!

Plate with click hinge

DECK DETAILS

Attach the mast with hinged plates so you can position it at an angle like it's been snapped at the base. A black ladder among the brown bricks adds interest and creates a really wrecked look!

HALF A SHIP

Once you know how to construct a ship, a wrecked one is easy—just build it partway! Make the edges of the hull uneven and add deck plates of different lengths so they look like boards smashed up by rocks in a storm.

ROWBOAT

Build a rowboat just like you would make a pirate ship, but on a smaller scale. Use a rectangular brick or plate across two 1x2 bricks to make the pirate's seat.

NOW THE TREASURE'S ALL...OOPS, I FORGOT TO TAKE THE TREASURE!

Oars attached to clips that move back and forth

You could perch a parrot on the prow!

Flagpole, made from antenna. You could attach a small sail or pirate flag

You could use bricks in different colors for a patchwork boat made from salvaged materials!

TOP VIEW

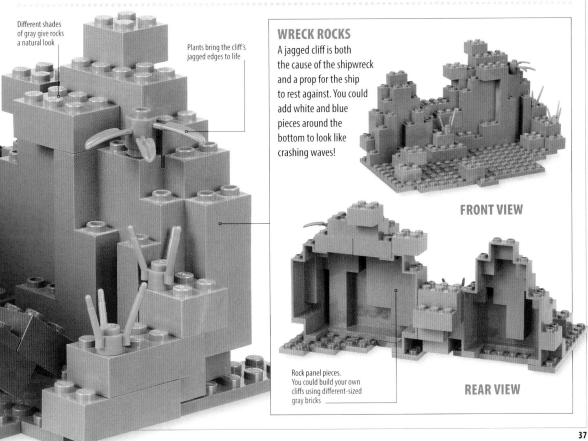

Different shades of gray give rocks a natural look

Plants bring the cliff's jagged edges to life

WRECK ROCKS

A jagged cliff is both the cause of the shipwreck and a prop for the ship to rest against. You could add white and blue pieces around the bottom to look like crashing waves!

FRONT VIEW

Rock panel pieces. You could build your own cliffs using different-sized gray bricks

REAR VIEW

PIRATE ISLAND

Even the most hardy sea dogs need somewhere to call home! Expand your pirate play with a pirate island. Imagine you're a pirate and think about what you might need in a hideout: How about a lookout for spotting enemy soldiers on the horizon? Or somewhere to moor your ship, or hide your treasure?

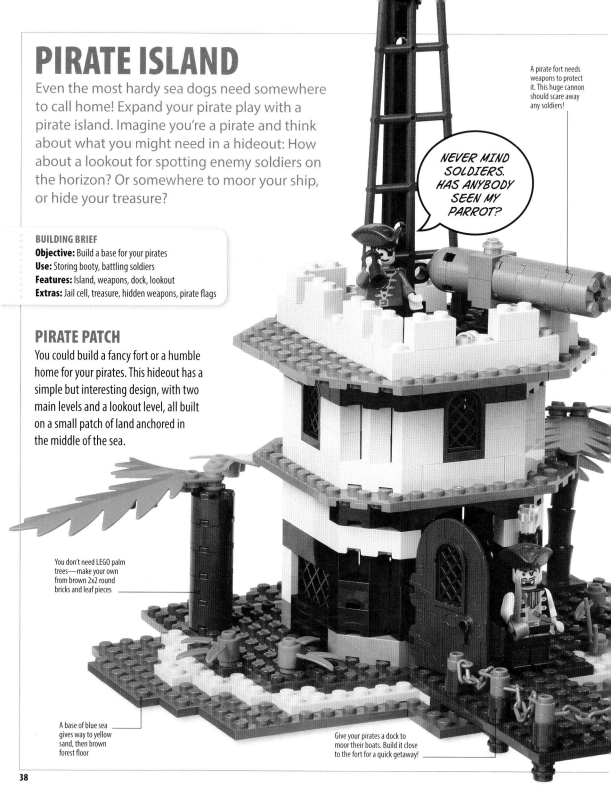

> **BUILDING BRIEF**
> **Objective:** Build a base for your pirates
> **Use:** Storing booty, battling soldiers
> **Features:** Island, weapons, dock, lookout
> **Extras:** Jail cell, treasure, hidden weapons, pirate flags

PIRATE PATCH

You could build a fancy fort or a humble home for your pirates. This hideout has a simple but interesting design, with two main levels and a lookout level, all built on a small patch of land anchored in the middle of the sea.

A pirate fort needs weapons to protect it. This huge cannon should scare away any soldiers!

NEVER MIND SOLDIERS. HAS ANYBODY SEEN MY PARROT?

You don't need LEGO palm trees—make your own from brown 2x2 round bricks and leaf pieces

A base of blue sea gives way to yellow sand, then brown forest floor

Give your pirates a dock to moor their boats. Build it close to the fort for a quick getaway!

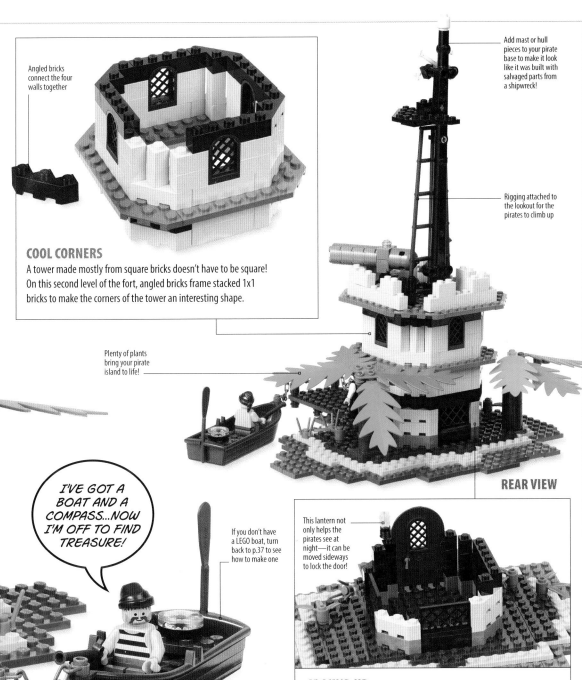

Angled bricks connect the four walls together

COOL CORNERS

A tower made mostly from square bricks doesn't have to be square! On this second level of the fort, angled bricks frame stacked 1x1 bricks to make the corners of the tower an interesting shape.

Add mast or hull pieces to your pirate base to make it look like it was built with salvaged parts from a shipwreck!

Rigging attached to the lookout for the pirates to climb up

Plenty of plants bring your pirate island to life!

REAR VIEW

I'VE GOT A BOAT AND A COMPASS...NOW I'M OFF TO FIND TREASURE!

If you don't have a LEGO boat, turn back to p.37 to see how to make one

This lantern not only helps the pirates see at night—it can be moved sideways to lock the door!

GROUND UP

The ground level features a large doorway and windows made from lattice fences. Dark tan bricks show where the tower has become dirty from the brown forest floor. Pirates aren't known for their cleanliness!

MEET THE BUILDER

DEBORAH HIGDON

Location: Canada
Age: 52
LEGO Specialty: Architecture, furniture

Which model were you most proud of as a young LEGO builder?

I don't remember being particularly proud of one model, but I do remember building houses—I loved the roof pieces and the doors and windows. In a box of things from my childhood, I still have pieces of a large fireplace that I built for my dolls, with candlesticks and a hand-drawn fire. I didn't like playing with dolls as much as I liked building furniture and houses for them!

This is a model of some buildings in the French village of St Paul de Vence. It was my first MOC to win a big competition at a LEGO fan festival.

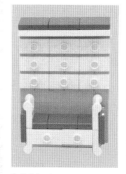

This little bench was built after I saw a picture of a real bench in a Dutch museum. I liked the style and color and thought I could model it in LEGO bricks.

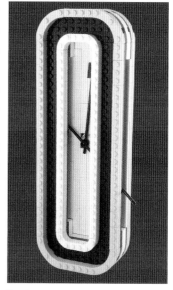

This MOC is based on a modern design I saw on the internet. I changed the colors and some parts of the design to make it work in LEGO bricks. And yes, it really does tell the time!

What is the biggest or most complex model you've made?

Mechanically, a sliding house was the most complex. It appeared to be a huge challenge but it was a simple solution in the end. I hid a motor in the "basement" and had the sliding roof of the house simply sit in a channel and be dragged along. At first, I thought of all kinds of complicated ways to get it to slide, but an AFOL (Adult Fan Of LEGO) friend and I talked about it, and he helped me come up with that simple solution. It doesn't always have to be complicated, sometimes we just think it does!

What is your favorite LEGO brick or piece?

That's really hard to choose but I think my favorite LEGO pieces are tiles. I wish they were all made in every color, every size! I like them because they really help to make a smooth piece of furniture look almost real. They also help to add small details, which are important when modeling houses and furniture.

If you had all the LEGO bricks (and time!) in the world, what would you build?

I've got a lot of ideas in my head so I don't know where I'd start! On my list of MOCs (My Own Creations) to do, there's a minifigure scale Garden of Versailles in France with all the buildings, fountains, and flower beds. I have also thought about a minifigure scale of a Greek fishing village in a mountain like the microscale one I made. But I'd need more than all the LEGO bricks and time in the world—I'd need a new house with an enormous LEGO room and the largest building table in the world!

What things have gone wrong and how have you dealt with them?

Things have fallen apart because I didn't build them strongly enough, especially when I have to travel with my MOCs. Occasionally, things fall on the floor and I have to rebuild them but sometimes I can't remember how I solved a particular problem so I have to rethink. I'm determined to make my ideas work. It takes a lot of patience and determination to rebuild, but it will always be worth it in the end. Often it turns out better than the original!

Another doorway from the series. I thought this could be the entrance to an old castle or manor house.

I tried building just doorways so that I could try different architectural styles without making the whole building. A gray stone doorway like this would be attached to a very big old stone house.

Microscale Rialto Bridge: this famous bridge crosses a canal in Venice, Italy. I wanted to build something like it and I wanted it to look like marble or very white stone, so I used just one color

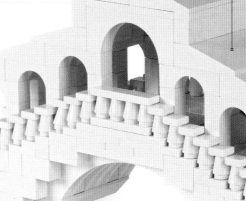

> I LIKE LOOKING AT VERY ORIGINAL FURNITURE AND THINKING OF HOW I CAN MODEL IT.

What are some of your top LEGO tips?

I think it's important to just play with putting bricks together, not even building anything: two little pieces you put together can suddenly look a bit like something you've seen elsewhere and may give you a brilliant idea for a creation. Look for interesting ways to connect two pieces and find out what fits together. Another good idea is to look at a lot of pictures if you're going to build something in model or replica. Getting tricky bricks apart is much easier with two brick separators—that's an important tip for everyone!

What else do you enjoy making apart from houses/buildings?

I've started to build some small sculptures and useful items like LEGO bookends, a clock, and a birdhouse. My first 3-D sculpture was a heart for Valentine's Day and I really enjoyed the challenge of forming the heart to get the curves just right.

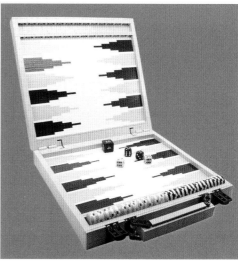

I was starting to build things that weren't houses and furniture so I thought I could start making useful things. I'd never seen a backgammon game made from LEGO pieces so I wanted it to be portable and playable, and it is.

How much time do you spend building?

When I'm in the middle of a project, full of ideas, I spend most evenings and weekends building, which is probably about 10–14 hours a week, sometimes more. At other times I don't build anything for weeks.

This model was built specially for this book. I looked carefully for pieces that could be the "hands" of the clock and I wanted the clock tower to look a little old-fashioned

Do you plan out your build? If so, how?

Only in my head! I think of one central feature of my new MOC (for example, the swimming pool, the main staircase, or the roof line) and I'll build the rest of the model around it. I make up my mind as I go along. Sometimes, I'll quickly do a rough sketch of a small part of a building I've seen, then I think of other things I can add to that feature. Sometimes I take pictures to remind me of a nice staircase, porch, or window I've seen that I'd like to try to replicate.

What is your favorite LEGO technique or technique you use the most?

I use a lot of hinges, especially the old finger hinges and I like to use LEGO Technic pieces to make interesting furniture. I also love to use a lot of SNOT (a LEGO fan term meaning Studs Not On Top).

What are you inspired by?

Mostly architecture and design—cool building ideas that I see in real life and I want to try to build in LEGO bricks. I like looking at very original furniture and thinking of how I can model it.

My LEGO club often has building challenges. So, for the Valentine's Day challenge I wanted to build something with dark red brick. I also wanted to try some 3-D shaping and a heart seemed a good shape to work with. I also wanted to add frilly lace and a way to curve the square edges so the tooth plates and hinges helped a lot.

This bookend is another useful MOC idea, something that anyone anywhere can enjoy and use. The "books" were fun to build and I printed the titles on clear sticker paper. The building has a little hiding spot for something special.

What is your favorite creation?

This changes all the time, especially after I've just finished a big creation. I think my most favorite will always be St Paul de Vence: I visited that town in France a long time ago. One day I decided to make some of the buildings there in LEGO bricks. There were about seven buildings and I built a walled platform for them, but because they were all separate, I could change the look just by moving the buildings around. Each separate building had a different challenge, which made it more fun to build.

How old were you when you started using LEGO bricks?

I was about seven or eight when I was first introduced to LEGO bricks. I stopped building, like many kids do, but I started again as an adult when I bought LEGO sets for my nieces and nephews. I really started buying and building for myself when I was 40. Then I found the online LEGO community, joined a local club for adults, and started to display publicly and post my work on the internet.

MEET THE BUILDER

DUNCAN TITMARSH

Location: UK
Age: 40
LEGO Specialty: Mosaics

What is the biggest or most complex model you've made?

I made a large version of LEGO set #375. It was the first castle the LEGO Group ever made and was in yellow. To make it bigger I built all the bricks six times bigger—some were easy but there were a few more difficult bricks to make, such as the hinges. I was then able to assemble the set from the original instructions and make a very large castle.

My wife likes the artist Banksy's pictures, so I built this LEGO mosaic version of it for her. It hangs in our hallway at home.

This is another of my mosaics. I wanted to see what a flower would look like so I picked a daisy and built it using 9,216 1x1 plates.

How much time do you spend building?

Every day. I have turned my hobby into a job and I am one of only 13 LEGO® Certified Professionals in the world. I build larger-than-life creations for companies who want to promote their products. I also build family pictures from 1x1 plates to form LEGO mosaics.

I THINK I HAVE IN THE REGION OF 1,000,000 BRICKS!

What is your favorite LEGO brick or piece?

The 1x2 brick is my favorite brick because you can use it to build very big walls. You don't even need any 1x1 bricks as you can turn the 1x2 on its side to fill the gap. When building with these it gives a great looking brick wall effect. If you want to make a curved wall, add some round 1x1 bricks between the 1x2 bricks.

What is your favorite creation?

I made a mosaic of one of the artist Banksy's wall art. It took a couple of days to do but I think it looks great.

What are some of your top LEGO tips?

I always use a brick separator as it's made for the job and you don't break your fingernails or damage the bricks. If I have a LEGO Technic pin stuck in a beam, I use an axle to push from the other side.

What things have gone wrong and how have you dealt with them?

You can be working close up on a model and it seems alright, but when you stand back it's not quite right or you have missed some detail that could look better. The only thing to do is to take some of the model apart and rebuild it. You always feel better in the end, even though it takes longer.

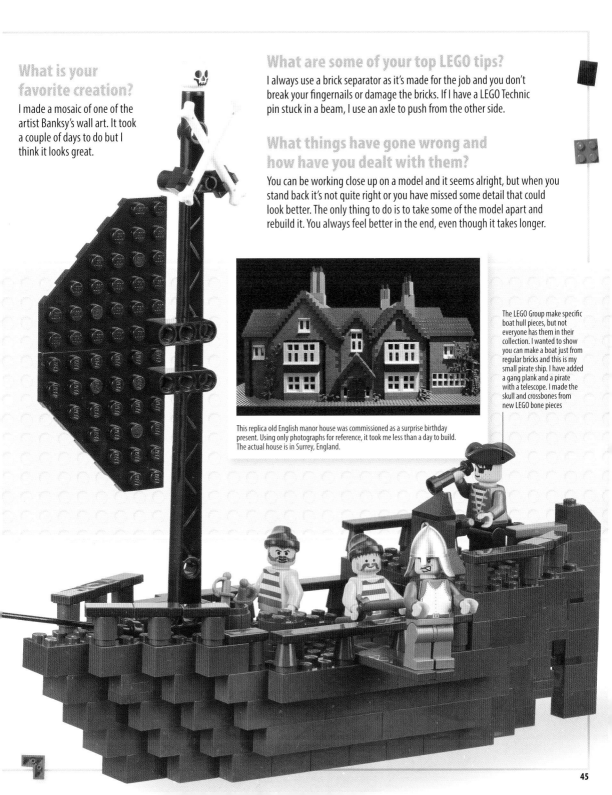

This replica old English manor house was commissioned as a surprise birthday present. Using only photographs for reference, it took me less than a day to build. The actual house is in Surrey, England.

The LEGO Group make specific boat hull pieces, but not everyone has them in their collection. I wanted to show you can make a boat just from regular bricks and this is my small pirate ship. I have added a gang plank and a pirate with a telescope. I made the skull and crossbones from new LEGO bone pieces

MEET THE BUILDER

SEBASTIAAN ARTS

Location: The Netherlands
Age: 27
LEGO Specialty: Castles and other medieval buildings

What are you inspired by?

I mostly make buildings, so I often get inspiration just walking around town. Whenever I watch documentaries or read articles about castles and medieval buildings, my fingers really itch to build! I also get a lot of inspiration from movies—I pay particular attention to the background buildings and scenery. Seeing LEGO creations by other builders is also a great source of inspiration: sometimes I'll see a clever building technique or part of a creation that makes me think, so I can't stop myself from sitting down and building.

Placing part of your building at an unusual angle can really make your castle a lot more interesting looking.

It's not all about castles! You can also build churches, houses, and farms in a medieval setting. This model is based on the church of Scherpenheuvel in Belgium.

To the walls! Siege towers like this were used very widely in the Middle Ages. Invaders could approach their enemy's castle walls protected in their siege tower and then use the height of the tower to climb up and over the castle walls.

If you had all the LEGO bricks (and time!) in the world, what would you build?

This is a subject that has come up in conversations with other fans many times before, and for me that's an easy answer. There's a castle on a rocky island in the north of France named Mont Saint-Michel. I would love to build that whole castle in full minifigure scale. That would be my dream creation.

NOTHING IS IMPOSSIBLE WITH LEGO BRICKS!

What is your favorite creation?

The "Abbey of Saint Rumare," a fictional fortified church built on a rock. It's big, complex, and full of different techniques and building styles—the landscape alone combines water with landscaping, rocky surfaces, and vegetation. The main structure has a huge church in tan, gray fortifications, and lots of different buildings inside in different colors and styles, to create that messy, thrown-together look that you would often find in medieval castles.

What things have gone wrong and how have you dealt with them?

My first response to any question like this would be that nothing is impossible with LEGO bricks! If you're building something that doesn't quite fit, there's always a different combination of parts that will fit. If you can't figure it out, step back for a bit, do something else, and go back to your "problem" later—you'll often suddenly see a solution.

What is the biggest or most complex model you've made?

The biggest model I've made is the "Abbey of Saint Rumare." This model was also quite complex, because everything is built at different angles. My most complex model by far was a star-shaped fort, which I named "Herenbosch." The star shape created a series of odd angles linked together, which then had to fit snugly with the buildings inside the castle. This took a lot of work—mostly trial and error—to find exactly the right angles for every part of the castle.

Height can add another dimension to your creation. A tall castle can look a lot more impressive than a bigger, more spread out one. This is my favorite creation, the Abbey of Saint Rumare.

How old were you when you started using LEGO bricks?

On my fourth birthday I received my first LEGO sets, and it all started there: I got hooked straightaway. For every birthday that followed, all I wanted was more LEGO sets. From an early age, I always enjoyed building my own creations.

A drawbridge can also be used as an effective door. However, you need to make it big enough to cover the gate when raised

DK

LONDON, NEW YORK
MELBOURNE, MUNICH, and DEHLI

Editor   Shari Last
Additional Editors   Simon Beecroft, Jo Casey, Hannah Dolan,
Emma Grange, Catherine Saunders, Lisa Stock, Victoria Taylor
Senior Editor   Laura Gilbert
Designer   Owen Bennett
Additional Designers   Guy Harvey, Lynne Moulding, Robert Perry,
Lisa Sodeau, Ron Stobbart, Rhys Thomas, Toby Truphet
Senior Designer   Nathan Martin
Design Manager   Ron Stobbart
Art Director   Lisa Lanzarini
Publishing Manager   Catherine Saunders
Publisher   Simon Beecroft
Publishing Director   Alex Allan
Production Editor   Sean Daly
Production Controller   Nick Seston

Photography by Gary Ombler,
Brian Poulsen, and Tim Trøjborg

This American Edition published in 2013
Contains content previously published in the United States in 2011 in
The LEGO® Ideas Book
001-194846 Sep/13

Published in the United States by DK Publishing
345 Hudson Street, New York, New York 10014

DK books are available at special discounts when purchased in bulk for sales promotions,
premiums, fund-raising, or educational use. For details, contact: DK Publishing Special
Markets, 375 Hudson Street, New York, New York 100014specialsales@dk.com.

A catalog record for this book is available from the Library of Congress.
ISBN: 978-1-4654-1367-3

Reproduced by MDP in the UK
Printed and bound in China by Leo Paper Products Ltd.

Discover more at
www.dk.com
www.LEGO.com

Acknowledgments

Dorling Kindersley would like to thank: Stephanie Lawrence,
Randi Sørensen, and Corinna van Delden at the LEGO Group;
Sebastiaan Arts, Deborah Higdon, and Duncan Titmarsh
(www.bright-bricks.com) for their amazing models; Jeff van
Winden for additional building; Daniel Lipkowitz for his fantastic
text; Gary Ombler, Brian Poulsen, and Tim Trøjborg for their
brilliant photography; Rachel Peng and Bo Wei at IM Studios;
and Sarah Harland for editorial assistance.